FIKA

———

Recipes for 30 baking classics.
From bite-size biscuits to festive cakes.

There's something primordial about baking.
We open a window into the past. A window
our modern lives tend to keep closed.
Like a wormhole through time.

Does the attraction lie in the actual creation?
In curbing our powers, being in complete
control? If I do my job, the oven will do the
same. And the rewards are just around the
corner.

A tray full of freshly baked favourites. Warm
aromas rising up and spreading out. Divine
coffee and refreshing squash being poured
into cups and glasses.

Calm gathers, time slows down. Slows right
down and stops awhile. Stops in this very
moment.

Welcome to *fika*!*

** Fika, a break for coffee and a bite to eat,
is a cornerstone of Swedish food culture.
A moment's relaxation with friends, family
or colleagues. There's no bad time, place
or situation for fika. Swedes grab every
opportunity!*

FIKA

Index

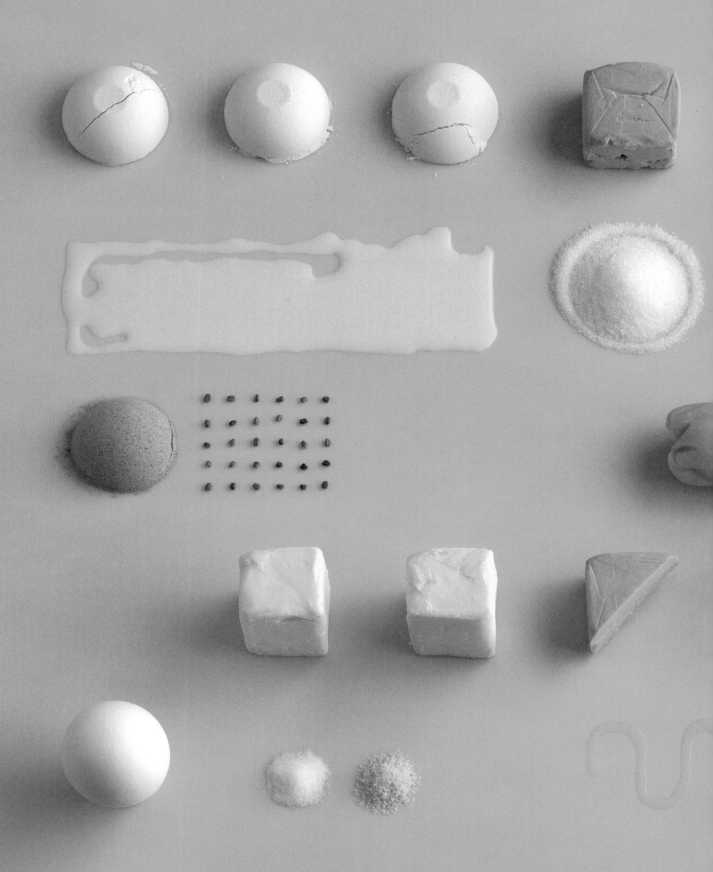

Ingredients:
75 g fresh yeast
500 ml milk
1.8-2 l plain flour
200 g butter
200 ml caster sugar
2 eggs
1 tsp salt
1 tbsp crushed cardamom

Cinnamon filling:
100 g marzipan
100 g butter
125 ml caster sugar
2½ tbsp dried breadcrumbs
1 tbsp water
1 tbsp cinnamon

Glaze and garnish:
1 egg
1 ml salt
½ tsp water
nib sugar

What to do:

1. Get out all the ingredients and let them reach room temperature.

2. Crumble the yeast into a food mixer or bowl. Pour over the milk (room temperature or heated until lukewarm, 37ºC) and stir until the yeast dissolves.

3. Add most of the flour, all of the butter in pieces, the sugar, eggs, salt and cardamom. Work the dough until very smooth, either in the mixer or by hand. Add extra flour if necessary. When the dough is smooth and the fat starts to ooze out, it's ready.

4. Leave the dough to rise under a baking cloth until it doubles in size, around 30 minutes.

5. Meanwhile, make the filling. Blend or whisk grated marzipan with the butter, sugar, bread-crumbs, water and cinnamon.

6. Place the dough onto a pastry board, knead it and divide into two. Roll each piece into a large rectangle. Spread with the cinnamon filling.

7. Roll the pastry up from the long side. Brush the edge with a little water to help it stick. Cut into 2-3 cm pieces. Place on trays lined with baking paper, leaving space to expand.

8. Leave to rise under a baking cloth until they double in size, around 20-30 minutes. Pre-heat the oven to 250ºC.

9. Whisk together the egg, salt and water and gently brush the mixture onto the buns. Sprinkle with the nib sugar. Bake in the middle of the oven for 7-8 minutes.

9

Ingredients:

75 g fresh yeast

500 ml milk

2.2-2.4 l (approx. 1.33 kg)
plain flour

200 g butter

250 ml caster sugar

2 eggs

1 tsp salt

Saffron syrup:

50 ml water

50 ml (just over) caster sugar

1 g saffron

Glaze and garnish:

raisins

1-2 eggs

1 ml salt

½ tsp water

What to do:

1. Let all the ingredients reach room temperature. Bring the water and sugar for the syrup to the boil and simmer for a minute or so. Remove the saucepan from the heat and stir in the saffron. Leave to cool.

2. Crumble the yeast into a food mixer or bowl. Pour over the milk (room temperature or heated until lukewarm, 37ºC) and stir until the yeast dissolves.

3. Add most of the flour, all of the butter in pieces, the sugar, eggs, salt and saffron syrup. Work the dough thoroughly, either in the mixer or by hand (at least 5 minutes). Add extra flour if necessary and continue to work the dough until it's smooth and shiny.

4. Leave the dough to rise under a baking cloth until it doubles in size, at least 30 minutes.

5. Place the dough onto a pastry board, knead it and divide into 35-40 pieces (around 60 or 70 g each).

6. Roll the pieces into narrow lengths of about 25 cm. Roll in two stages, leaving in between to avoid cracking. Roll the ends in opposite ways to form S-shapes. Place on a tray lined with baking paper. Press in the raisins.

7. Leave to rise under a baking cloth until they double in size, at least 30 minutes. Pre-heat the oven to 250ºC.

8. Whisk together the egg, salt and water and brush the mixture onto the buns. Bake in the middle of the oven for around 5 minutes.

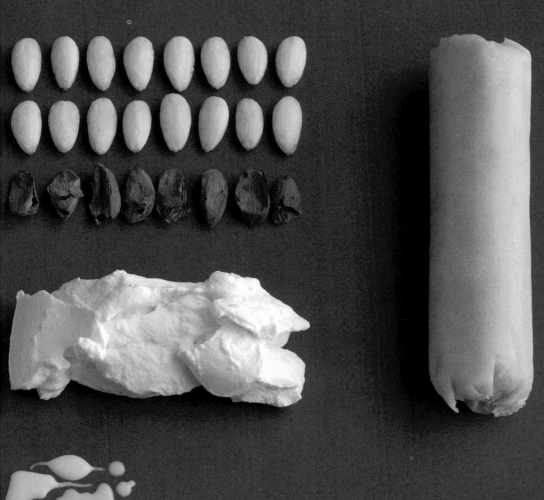

Ingredients:

1.4-1.6 l (approx. 1 kg)
  strong flour
150 ml caster sugar
125 g butter
  (room temperature)
50 g fresh yeast
2 tsp crushed cardamom
1 egg
500 ml milk

Glaze:

2 egg yolks
1-2 tbsp milk

Filling:

100 g blanched almonds
crumbs from the buns
approx. 50 ml milk
250 g marzipan

Garnish:

400-500 ml whipped cream
icing sugar

1. Mix most of the flour, the sugar, butter in pieces, crumbled yeast, cardamom and egg in a bowl or food mixer.

2. Heat the milk to 37°C, luke-warm, and pour it over the mixture. Work the dough thoroughly for around 10 minutes until it is smooth and shiny, and comes away from the edge of the bowl. Leave to rise under a baking cloth for 30-40 minutes.

3. Place the dough onto a floured pastry board and knead gently. Divide the dough into 20 or 40 pieces and roll into smooth buns. Place on a tray lined with baking paper.

4. Leave to rise under a baking cloth for 30-40 minutes. Pre-heat the oven to 225°C.

5. Whisk together the egg yolks with a little milk and carefully brush over the buns. Bake in the oven for 7-10 minutes. Leave to cool on a cooling rack.

6. Filling: Pre-heat the oven to 175°C. Toast the blanched almonds lightly in the oven for 10-15 minutes until they gain just a little colour. Leave to cool and chop coarsely.

7. Cut the top off the buns and scoop out some of the crumbs from each. Using an electric whisk or food processor, mash the crumbs with the milk, grate in the marzipan and work into a smooth, even paste. Finally, fold in the almonds.

8. Preparing the buns: Pipe the marzipan filling into the buns, and pipe the cream to cover the cut and the almond filling. Top with the hat and sprinkle with icing sugar.

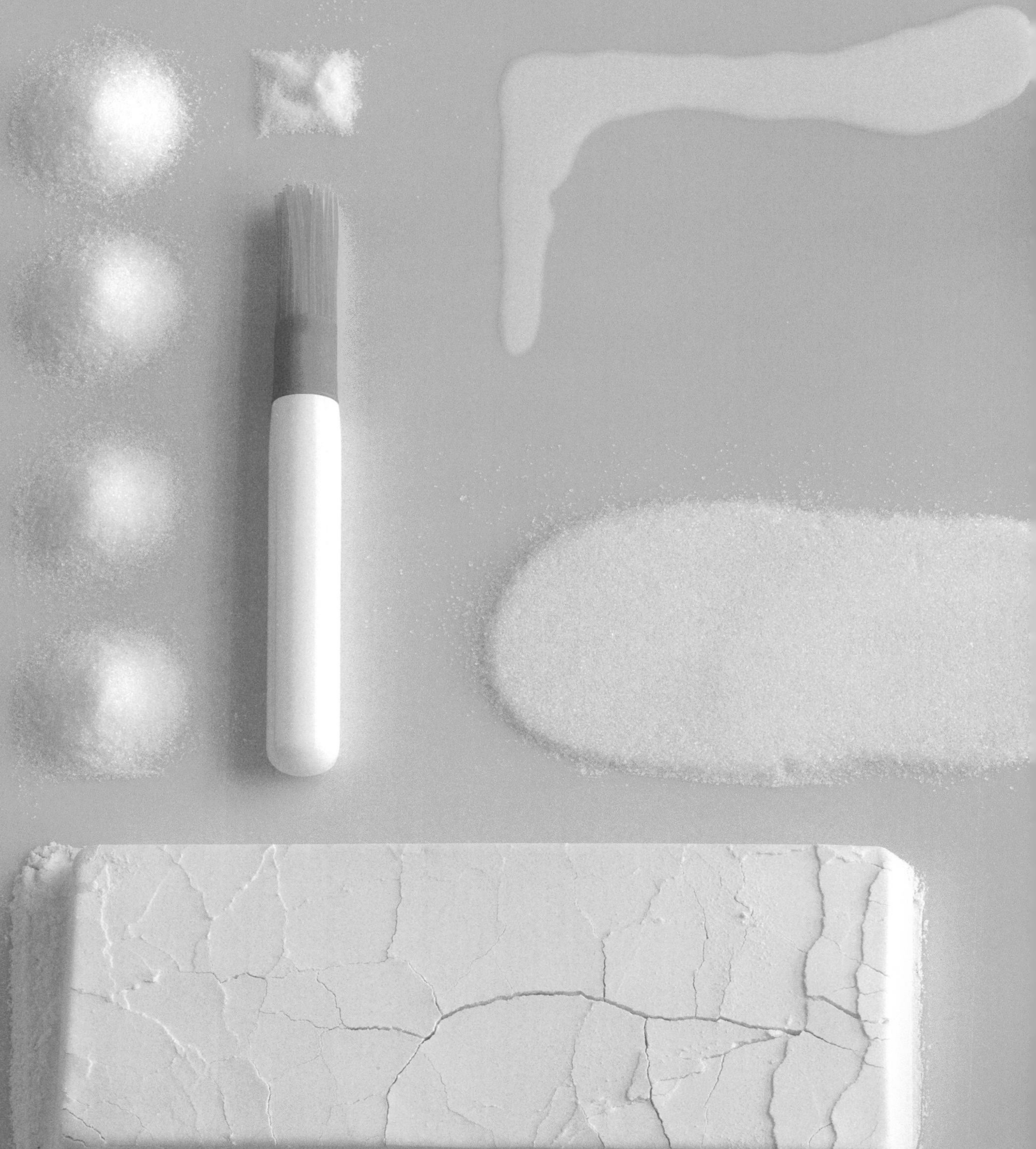

Ingredients:
750 ml plain flour
75 g butter
  (room temperature)
4 tbsp caster sugar
1 ml salt
1 egg
25 g fresh yeast
250 ml milk (37°C)

Vanilla cream filling:
150 ml single cream
1½ tbsp plain flour
½ tbsp caster sugar
1 egg
3 drops vanilla extract

Garnish:
approx. 25 g melted butter
approx. 100 ml caster sugar

What to do:

1. Put the flour, the butter in pieces, sugar, salt and egg into a food mixer bowl. Crumble over the yeast. Pour on the lukewarm milk and work the dough for a few minutes until it's smooth and comes away from the edge of the bowl.

2. Leave to rise under a baking cloth until the dough doubles in size, around 30 minutes.

3. Vanilla cream: Mix the cream, flour and sugar in a saucepan. Simmer the mixture over a low heat for about 3 minutes, stirring constantly. Remove the pan from the heat and mix in the egg. Carefully heat the cream again for about half a minute. Leave to cool and add the vanilla extract.

4. Place the dough onto a floured pastry board and knead gently. Divide the dough into 18 pieces and roll into smooth buns.

5. Flatten the buns with a rolling pin. Place 2 tsp vanilla cream on each. Pinch the buns closed and place them pinched side down onto a tray lined with baking paper.

6. Leave to rise under a baking cloth for 30-45 minutes. When the dough rises after a gentle press with the finger, it's ready. Meanwhile, pre-heat the oven to 225°C.

7. Bake in the middle of the oven for 7-8 minutes until the buns start to brown.

8. Leave to cool on a cooling rack. Glaze the buns with melted butter just before serving, and then roll them in caster sugar.

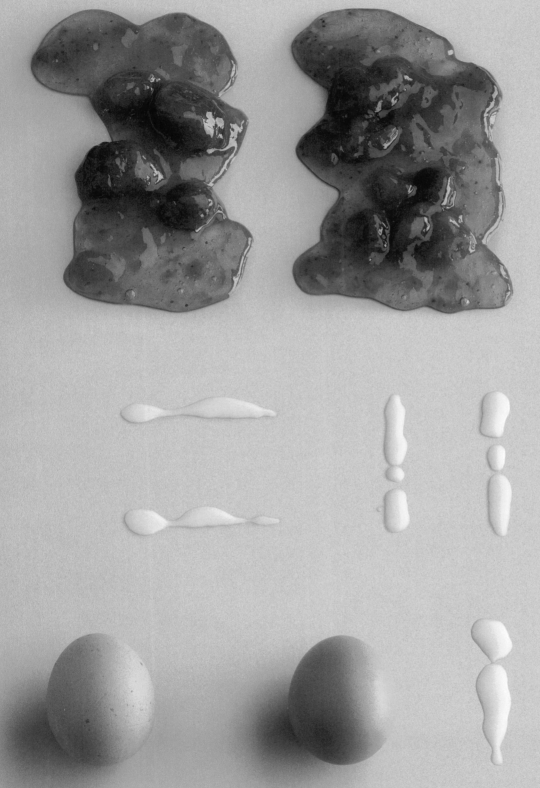

Ingredients:
3 eggs
200 ml caster sugar
200 ml plain flour
2 tsp baking powder
50 ml milk

Filling:
150 ml jam or pulped fruit

SWISS ROLL

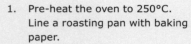
What to do:

1. Pre-heat the oven to 250°C. Line a roasting pan with baking paper.

2. Beat the eggs and sugar until light and fluffy.

3. Mix the flour and baking powder. Carefully stir into the egg mixture and add the milk. Stir into an even mixture.

4. Spread the mixture out in the roasting pan. Immediately bake in the bottom of the oven for around 5 minutes.

5. Sprinkle a little sugar over the cake and immediately turn it out onto baking paper or a cloth. Remove the oven paper. If the paper won't come loose, brush with a little cold water.

6. Spread the filling (jam or fruit pulp) over the warm cake, roll it together and stand with the join facing down. Cut into slices of the required size.

Tip:
Make individual Swiss roll cream cakes by cutting the cake into thicker slices and decorating with whipped cream and jam, fruit or berries.

Ingredients:

75 g butter

2 eggs

200 ml caster sugar

150 ml soured cream

300 ml plain flour

1½ tsp bicarbonate of soda

½ tsp ground cinnamon

½ tsp ground ginger

1 tsp ground cloves

30 g chopped pickled orange
  peel

100 ml set lingonberry jam

1. Grease a baking tin of about 1½ litres or line it with baking paper. Pre-heat the oven to 175°C.
2. Melt the butter and leave to cool.
3. Beat the eggs and sugar until light and fluffy. Add the soured cream.
4. Mix the flour, bicarbonate of soda, spices and orange peel, and add this to the mixture.
5. Add the lingonberry jam and finally the cooled butter. Pour the mixture into the tin.
6. Bake in the oven for 45-55 minutes. Turn the cake out onto a cooling rack and leave to cool under a baking cloth.

Ingredients:

2 eggs

200 ml caster sugar

275 ml plain flour

2 tsp baking powder

50 g melted butter

100 ml milk

1-2 drops vanilla extract or the
zest of 1 lemon (well washed)

What to do:

1. Pre-heat the oven to 175°C. Grease a 1½ litre baking tin or line it with baking paper.

2. Beat the eggs and sugar until pale, light and fluffy.

3. Mix the flour and baking powder and add this to the mixture.

4. Add the melted butter mixed with the milk and the vanilla extract or lemon zest. Stir carefully into an even mixture. Pour the mixture into the tin.

5. Bake at the bottom of the oven for about 40 minutes.

Tip:

Chocolate cake: bake as above but replace the vanilla extract/ lemon zest with 3 tbsp cocoa powder (and mix the cocoa powder with the flour and baking powder, in step 3) and 3 drops vanilla extract. Reduce the flour to 250 ml.

Orange cake: bake as above but replace the milk with the same amount of freshly squeezed orange juice, and replace the vanilla extract/ lemon zest with the zest of 1 orange.

Ingredients:

200 g butter

200 g dark chocolate

2 eggs

200 ml chocolate flavour icing
 sugar

1 drop vanilla extract

approx. 25 plain biscuits such
 as Marie biscuits

What to do:

1. Line a loaf tin with foil or cling film.

2. Melt the butter and chocolate in a bowl in the microwave, or over a very low heat in a pan on the hob.

3. Beat the eggs, chocolate flavour icing sugar and vanilla extract until light and fluffy. Add the melted butter and chocolate to the egg mixture.

4. Spread a layer of chocolate mix at the bottom of the tin. Add a layer of biscuits on top of the chocolate mix. Then alternate chocolate mix and biscuits until the mix runs out. The final layer should be chocolate mix.

5. Refrigerate the cake for at least an hour.

6. Cut the cake into slices with a sharp knife.

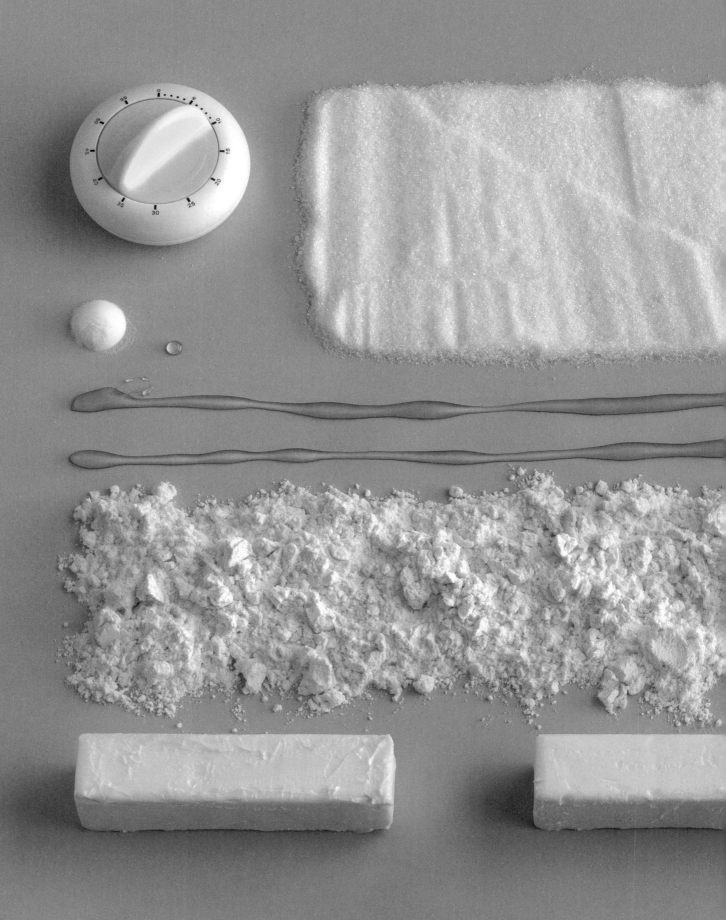

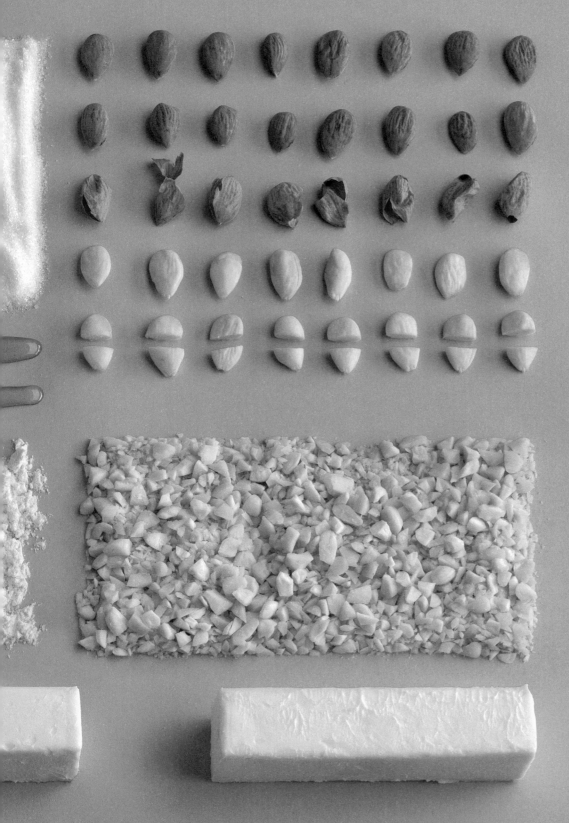

Ingredients:

100 g butter
  (room temperature)

100 ml caster sugar

1 tbsp syrup

50 ml (about 35 g) almonds

225 ml plain flour

½ tsp bicarbonate of soda

What to do:

1. Mix the butter, sugar and syrup into a smooth paste.

2. Blanche the almonds if necessary to remove the skin. Chop coarsely. Mix the almonds, flour and bicarbonate of soda. Add the almond mixture to the butter and work into a dough.

3. Roll the dough out into a roll approx. 3 cm thick. Wrap it in cling film and refrigerate for at least half an hour. (Ideally leave it longer. It can also be frozen.) Pre-heat the oven to 200°C.

4. Remove the cling film, cut the roll with a sharp knife into slices approx. 1 cm thick and lay out on a tray lined with baking paper. Bake in the middle of the oven for 6-8 minutes. Leave the biscuits to cool on the paper or a cooling rack.

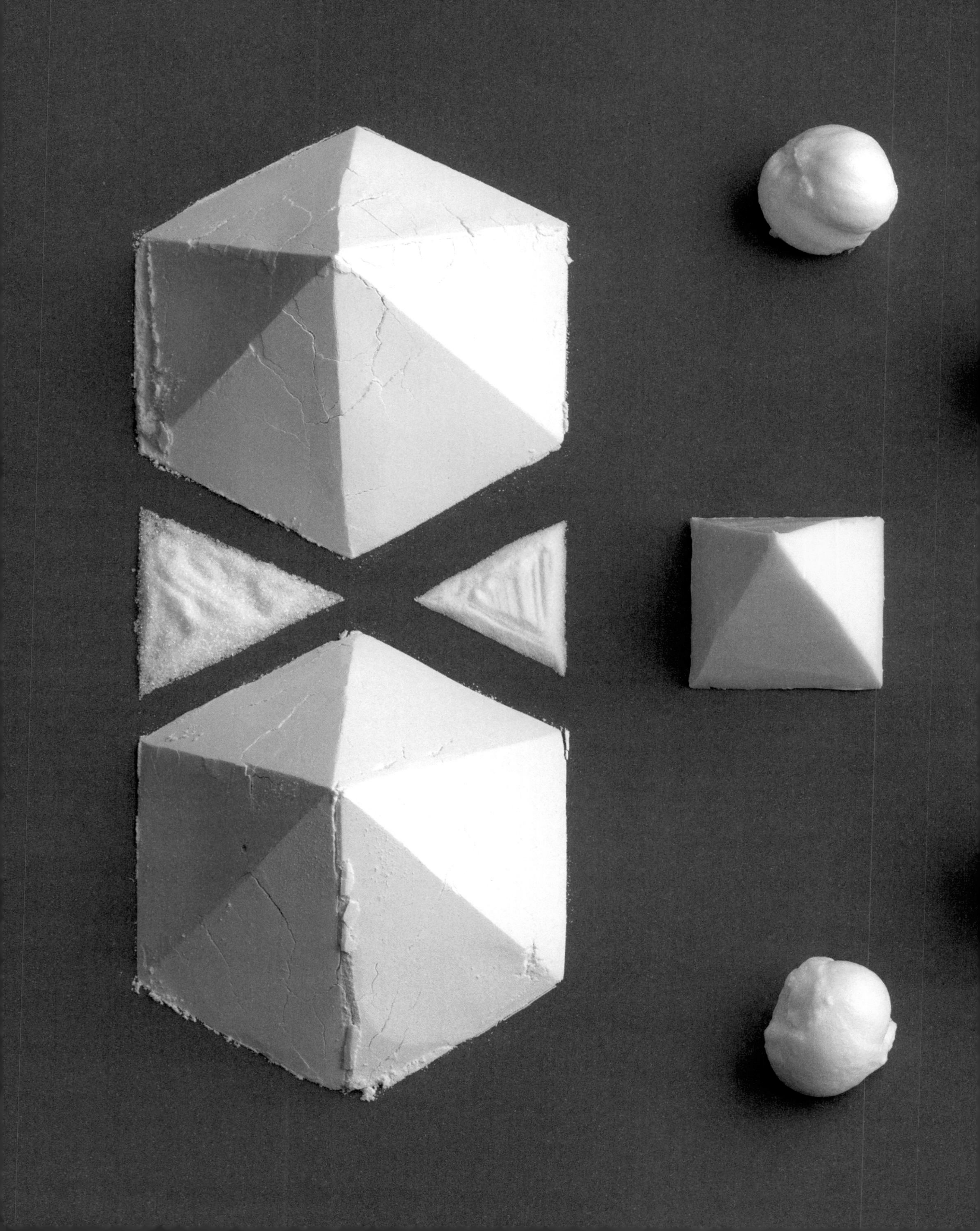

Ingredients:

900 ml plain flour

1 tbsp ammonium carbonate

200 ml caster sugar

200 g butter

2 eggs

200 ml plain yogurt or soured
  cream

Flavouring:

2-3 drops bitter almond
  extract or zest of 1 lemon or 1
  tbsp crushed cardamom

Glaze and garnish:

beaten egg

nib sugar

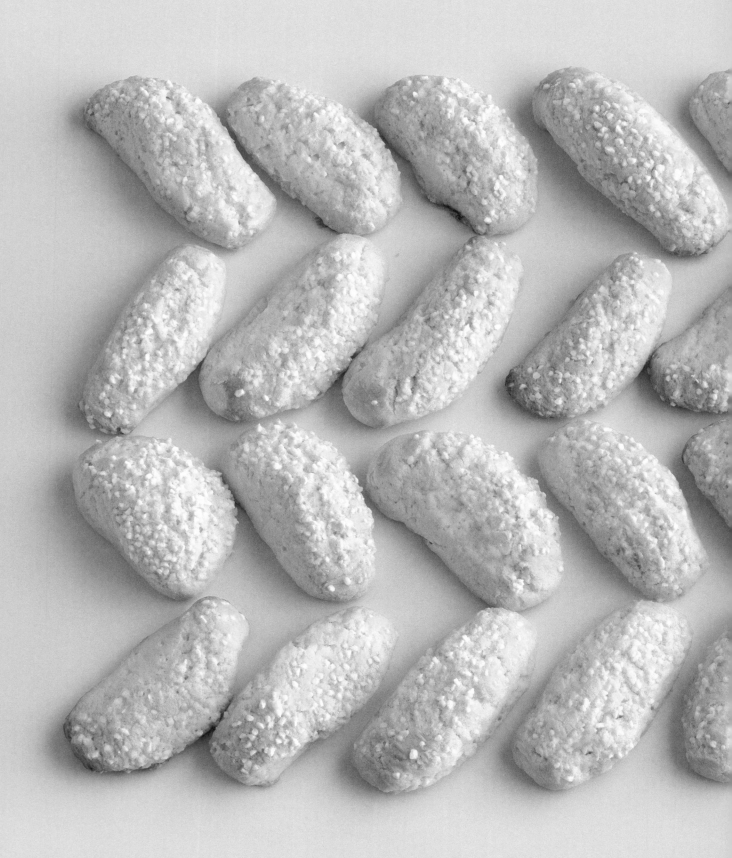

What to do:

1. Pre-heat the oven to 225°C.
2. Put the flour, ammonium carbonate and sugar into a bowl or food mixer. Add the butter in small pieces. Add the eggs, soured cream/plain yogurt and flavouring. Quickly mix into a dough (do it too slowly and the buns come out chewy). Stand for about 10 minutes.
3. Transfer the dough to a floured pastry board and roll out into two lengths.
4. Brush with egg. Dip each length into the nib sugar. Cut each length into about 18 pieces. Place on a tray lined with baking paper.
5. Bake in the middle of the oven for about 10 minutes.

Tip:
'Kubb' cakes are extra nice eaten freshly baked.

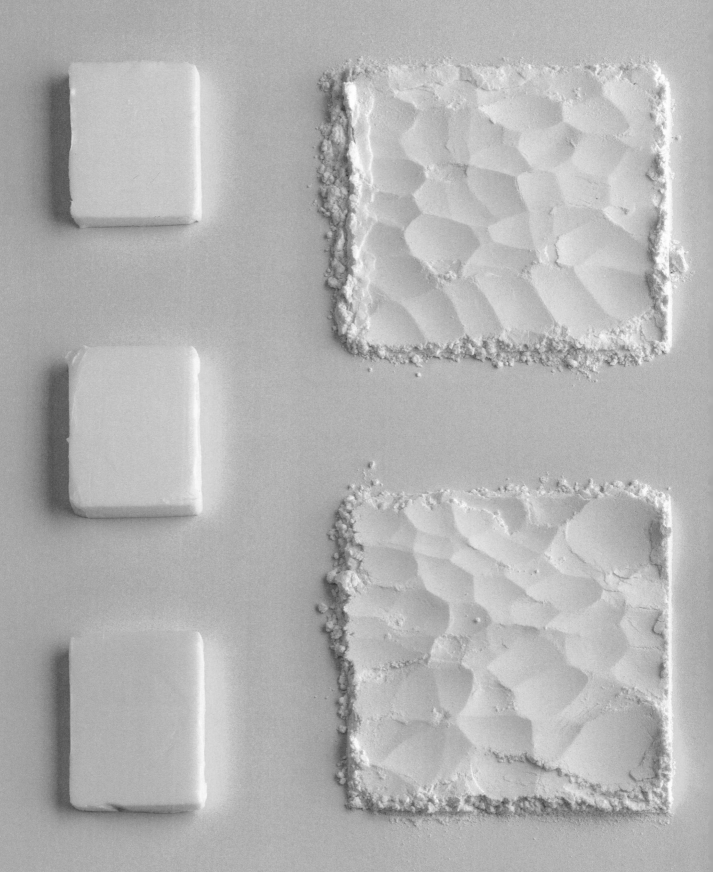

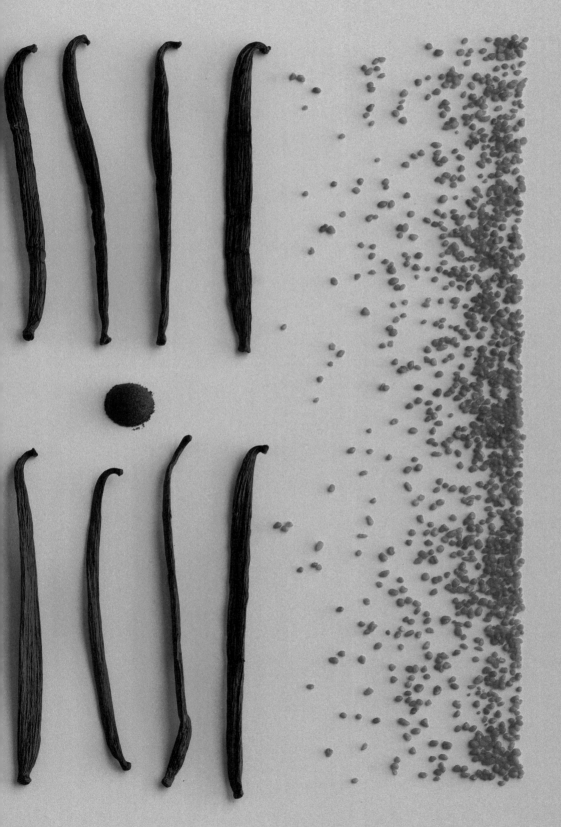

Ingredients:
350-400 ml plain flour
150 g butter
3 drops vanilla extract

Garnish:
3 tbsp strawberry pearls
  or some other sprinkles,
  or 50 ml caster sugar

What to do:

1. Pre-heat the oven to 175°C. Quickly mix the flour (save a little for shaping), butter and vanilla extract (can be done in a food processor). Refrigerate for a while.

2. Transfer the dough to a floured pastry board and divide into 40 pieces. Roll into narrow lengths of about 6 cm. They should be slightly thicker in the middle. Bend them into boomerangs and place on a tray lined with baking paper.

3. Bake in the oven for 8-10 minutes.

4. Roll the biscuits in sprinkles or sugar as soon as they come out of the oven.

Tip:
If the sprinkles or sugar come off before serving, you can quickly and gently heat the biscuits in the microwave and roll them in the garnish once again.

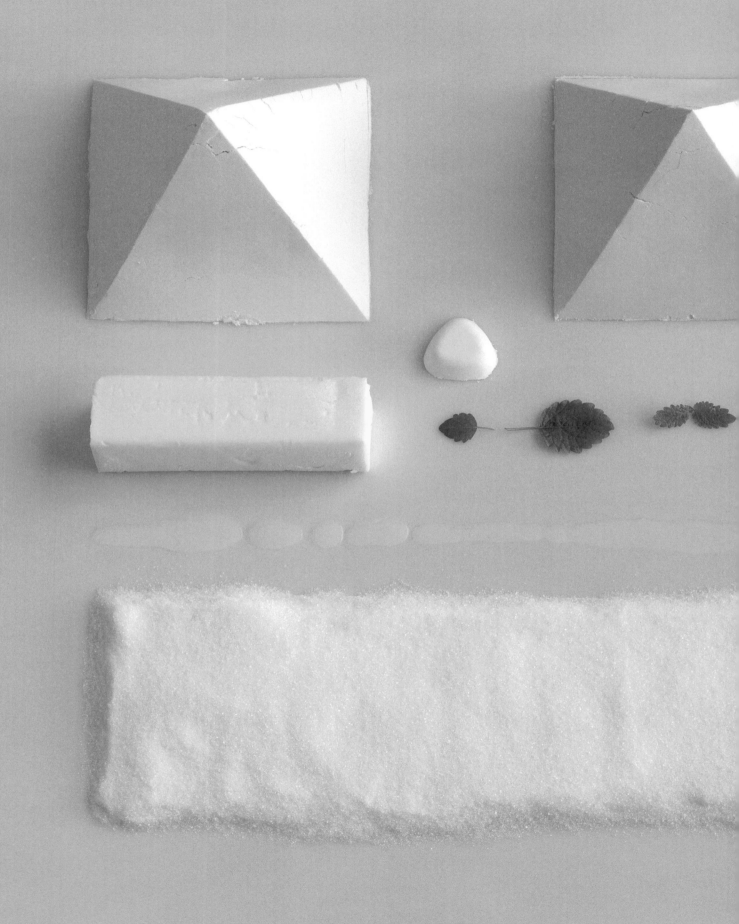

Ingredients:

50 g butter
(room temperature)

50 ml cooking oil
(neutral flavour)

150 ml caster sugar

250 ml plain flour

1 drop vanilla extract

½ tsp ammonium carbonate

1 bunch lemon balm leaves,
approx. 50 ml

1. Pre-heat the oven to 150°C. Mix the butter, oil and sugar until pale, light and fluffy.

2. Mix the flour and ammonium carbonate and add to the butter. Mix in the vanilla extract.

3. Chop the lemon balm leaves and fold them into the mixture.

4. Roll into small balls and place them on a tray lined with baking paper.

5. Bake in the middle of the oven for 12-15 minutes.

Ingredients:
225 ml plain flour
50 ml cocoa powder
100 g butter
50 ml caster sugar
½ an egg yolk

Filling:
1 egg white
100 ml caster sugar

1. Sift the flour and cocoa together. Mix with the butter, sugar and half egg yolk. Wrap the dough in cling film and refrigerate for at least an hour.

2. Between cling film or baking paper, roll out the dough into a sheet about 15×30 cm.

3. Beat the egg white into a foam. Add the sugar while beating and continue beating into a thick, creamy 'shaving foam'. If you do this over simmering water the foam is tougher and lasts better.

4. Spread the meringue mixture over the dough and roll up like a Swiss roll. Roll into cling film, place on a chopping board and leave to stand in the fridge for about 15 minutes. Pre-heat the oven to 175°C.

5. Remove the cling film and cut the dough into slices of 1 cm with a sharp knife. Place on a tray lined with baking paper. Bake for 10-12 minutes.

Ingredients:
approx. 600 ml plain flour
½ tsp baking powder
zest of ½ a lemon
133 ml caster sugar
50 g butter
2 eggs
125 ml whipping cream

Deep frying and garnish:
approx. 800 ml neutral cooking
  oil, such as rapeseed oil
approx. 100 ml caster sugar

What to do:

1. Mix half the flour with the baking powder, lemon zest and sugar.
2. Rub the cold butter into the flour mixture with your fingertips.
3. Beat the eggs with the cream and add this to the flour mixture.
4. Work in most of the remaining flour on the pastry board. Refrigerate in a plastic bag for a few hours.
5. Take a little at a time and roll the dough out thinly in a little flour, to about 20×30 cm.
6. Using a pastry wheel, cut into short lengths about 3 cm wide by 10 cm long. Make a slit into each piece. Thread one end through the slit and pull it so that the dough length becomes twisted.
7. Heat the oil to about 180°C. Deep fry a few crullers at a time until they turn golden yellow. This takes about 3 minutes. Turn them once with a fork while frying. Remove from the pan and drain them briefly onto kitchen roll.
8. Turn the crullers in sugar while they're hot.

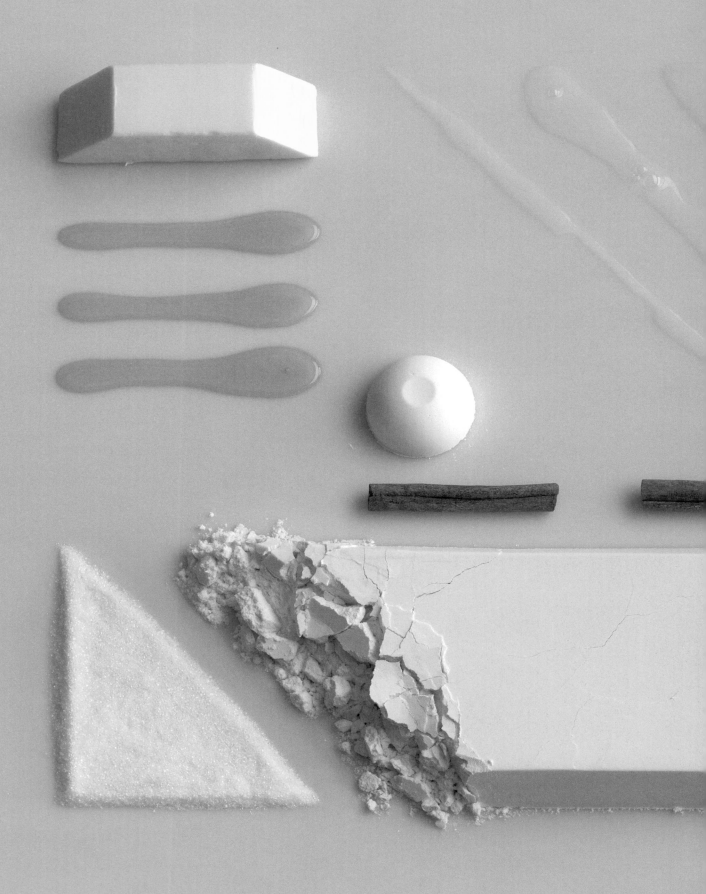

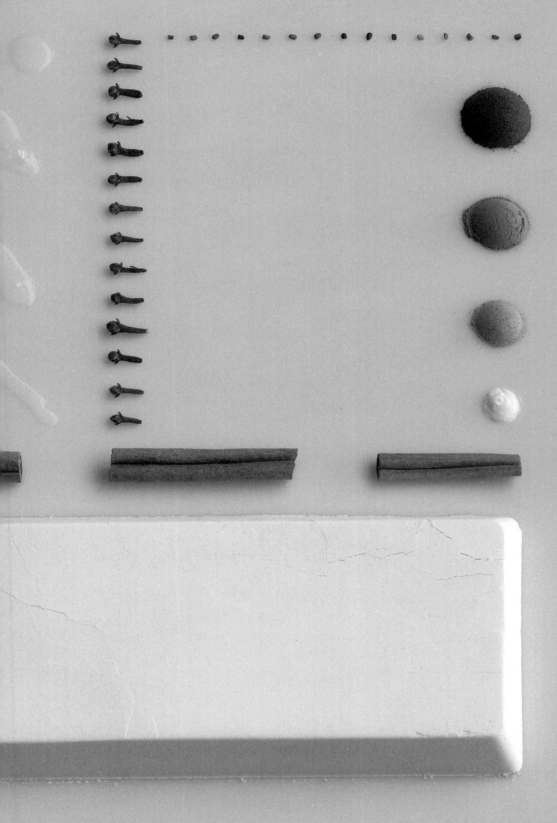

Ingredients:

200 ml caster sugar

100 ml golden syrup

100 ml water

125 g butter

1 tbsp cinnamon

½ tbsp ground cardamom

½ tbsp ground cloves

½ tbsp bicarbonate of soda

750 ml plain flour + a little
flour for rolling

Icing:

200 ml icing sugar

½ an egg white

1 ml vinegar or squeezed
lemon

food colourings

What to do:

1. Pour the sugar, syrup and water into a saucepan. Bring to the boil and remove from the heat.

2. Divide the butter and place in a bowl with the spices. Pour over the hot sugar mixture and mix until the butter has melted. Leave to cool to room temperature.

3. Mix the flour with the bicarbonate of soda and add this to the mixture, which is quite loose (it will rise later). Work the dough together.

4. Cover the bowl with plastic or put the dough in a plastic bag and leave to stand in the fridge for 24-48 hours.

5. Pre-heat the oven to 200°C. Lightly flour the pastry board and roll out a little dough at a time.

6. Use cutters to cut shapes and place on a tray lined with baking paper.

7. Bake in the oven for 4-6 minutes. Take care here – it's easy to burn gingerbread!

Icing:

Whisk all the icing ingredients together using an electric whisk. If you would like several different colours of icing, divide the mixture into several bowls and add drops of food colouring. Mix well and put the icing into different piping bags (available in most supermarkets). Close the bags with clips. Cut a small hole in the bag and decorate your gingerbread biscuits.

Ingredients:
100 g butter
100 ml caster sugar
1 tbsp syrup
250 ml plain flour
1 tsp baking powder
3 drops vanilla extract

What to do:

1. Pre-heat the oven to 175°C. Mix all the ingredients to a smooth dough in a bowl or food processor.

2. Roll out the dough into three finger-thick lengths, roughly as long as a baking tray. Place them on a tray lined with baking paper and flatten slightly.

3. Bake in the middle of the oven for around 12 minutes. Cut the lengths into diagonal biscuits while they're warm. Separate the biscuits once they've cooled.

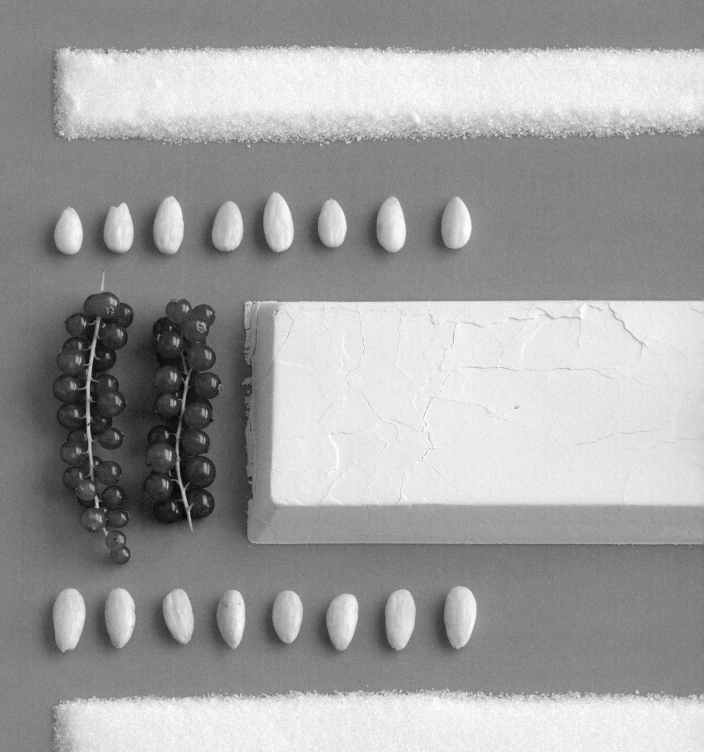

Ingredients:

500 ml plain flour

100 ml caster sugar

150 ml (100 g) blanched and
  peeled almonds

2 drops bitter almond extract

200 g butter
  (fridge temperature)

1 egg

individual fluted tart tins

1. Grease and flour the tart tins and lay them out on a tray. Mix the flour, sugar, almond, bitter almond extract and butter into a smooth paste in a food processor. Add the egg and mix it in.

2. Divide the dough into 3 pieces and roll into lengths. Wrap in cling film and refrigerate for 1-2 hours.

3. Pre-heat the oven to 175°C. Remove the mix from the fridge, remove the cling film and divide each roll into 12 pieces. Press the dough out in each tin with a floured thumb. Bake for 8-12 minutes. Turn the cups over when they have cooled somewhat and carefully remove the almond clams.

Tip:
Serve the almond clams as pastries with whipped cream and fresh berries, cloudberry jam or jelly.

Ingredients:

200 g butter

100 ml caster sugar

100 g ground hazelnuts

350-400 ml plain flour

Garnish:

approx. 100 g dark cooking
  chocolate

What to do:

1. Pre-heat the oven to 175°C.
2. Mix all the ingredients to a smooth dough in a bowl or food processor.
3. Roll the dough out into lengths just under finger thick. Cut into pieces 4-5 cm long and place on a tray lined with baking paper.
4. Bake in the middle of the oven for 12-18 minutes.
5. Break the chocolate into bits and melt in the microwave or over a pan of simmering water.
6. When the cigars have cooled off, dip one end in the melted chocolate. Leave to set on baking paper.

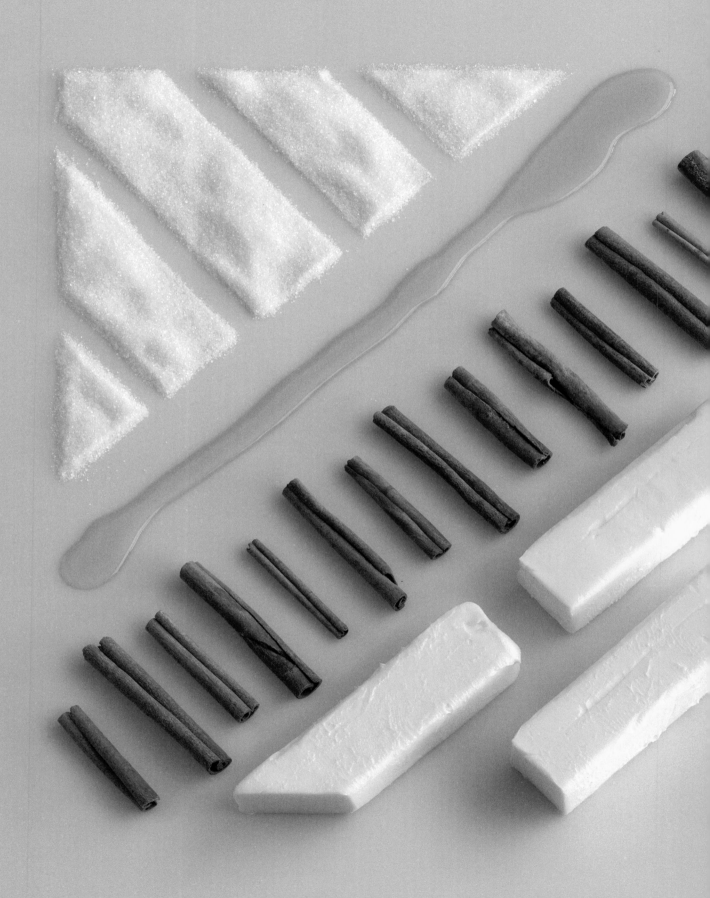

Ingredients:

200 g butter

100 ml caster sugar

1½ tbsp syrup

2 tsp cinnamon

1 tsp crushed cardamom

2 tsp bicarbonate of soda
dissolved in ½ tbsp lukewarm
water

400-450 ml plain flour

What to do:

1. Mix the butter, sugar, syrup, cinnamon, cardamom, bicarbonate solution and 400 ml of flour in a food processor. Add a bit extra flour if necessary. Pre-heat the oven to 175°C.

2. Divide the dough into quarters, and each quarter into 12 pieces. Roll each piece out to about 8 cm. Bend them into horseshoes and place on a tray lined with baking paper.

3. Flour a fork and press patterns into the horseshoes.

4. Bake in the oven for about 10 minutes.

Ingredients:

2 egg whites

100 ml caster sugar

4-5 drops lemon juice or vinegar

juice from raspberries (optional)

1. Pre-heat the oven to 100-125°C. Pour the egg whites into a fully clean and dry bowl. Beat the egg whites and lemon juice/vinegar into a firm foam. This takes at least 2 minutes with an electric whisk.

2. Add the sugar and stir carefully.

3. Spoon or pipe the mix into the desired shapes onto a tray lined with baking paper.

4. Cook the meringues in the middle of the oven until they're ready and come easily off the paper. This takes about 45-90 minutes. Leave to cool on a cooling rack.

Tip:
Flavour the meringues with berry juice. Raspberries add a nice colour. Drip a little juice into each meringue on the baking tray and stir with a teaspoon handle.

Ingredients:
200 g butter
100 ml caster sugar
2 drops vanilla extract
450-500 ml plain flour

Flavouring:
2 tbsp cocoa powder

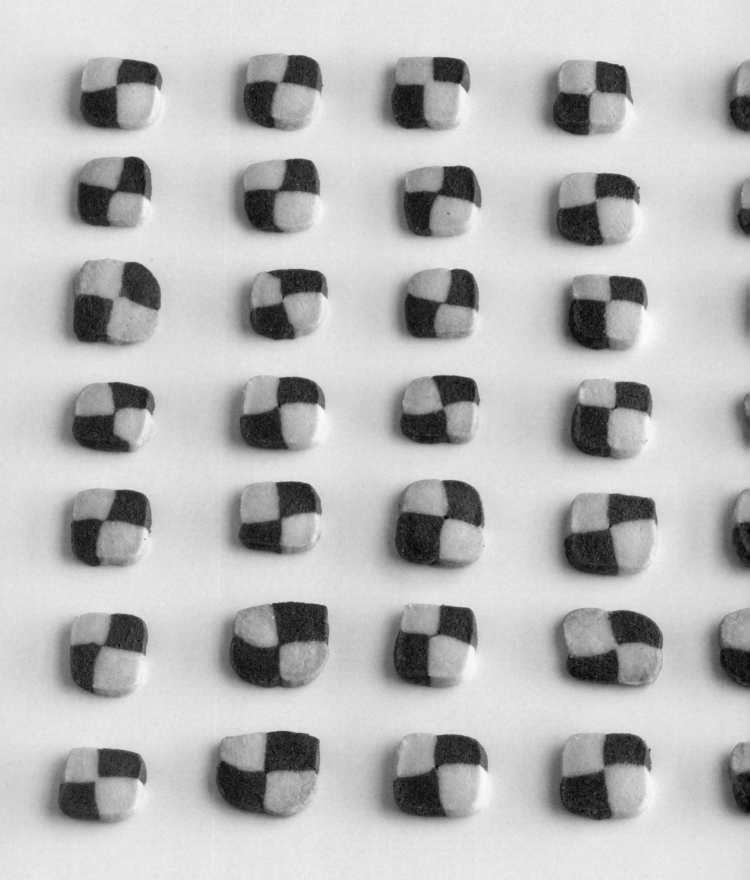

What to do:

1. Mix the butter, sugar, vanilla extract and flour. Quickly work into a smooth dough.

2. Divide the dough into two equal pieces.

3. Mix sifted cocoa into one half and possibly a little more flour into the other.

4. Divide both the light and the dark dough into two pieces. Roll out the four pieces into lengths about 1½ cm thick.

5. Place a light length next to a dark one, a dark on top of a light and a light on top of a dark. Press together slightly.

6. Wrap this in cling film and leave to set in the fridge for about an hour. Pre-heat the oven to 175°C.

7. Remove the cling film and cut the roll into slices 3-4 mm thick. Place on a tray lined with baking paper. Bake in the middle of the oven for 8-10 minutes.

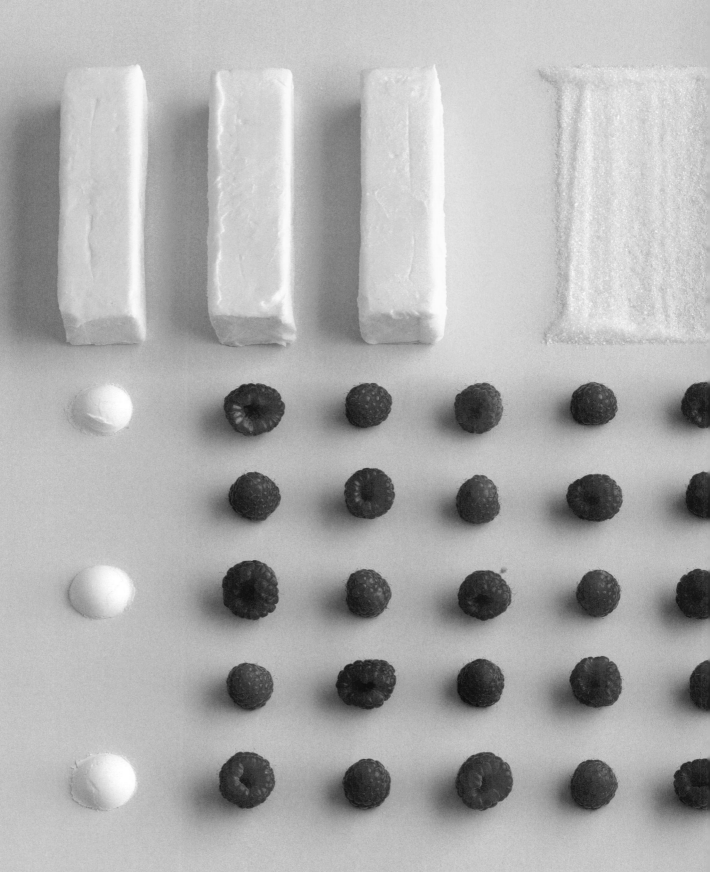

Ingredients:
125 g butter
  (room temperature)
75 ml caster sugar
200 ml plain flour
50 ml potato flour
2 drops vanilla extract
1 tsp baking powder

Filling and garnish:
50 ml set raspberry jam
icing sugar

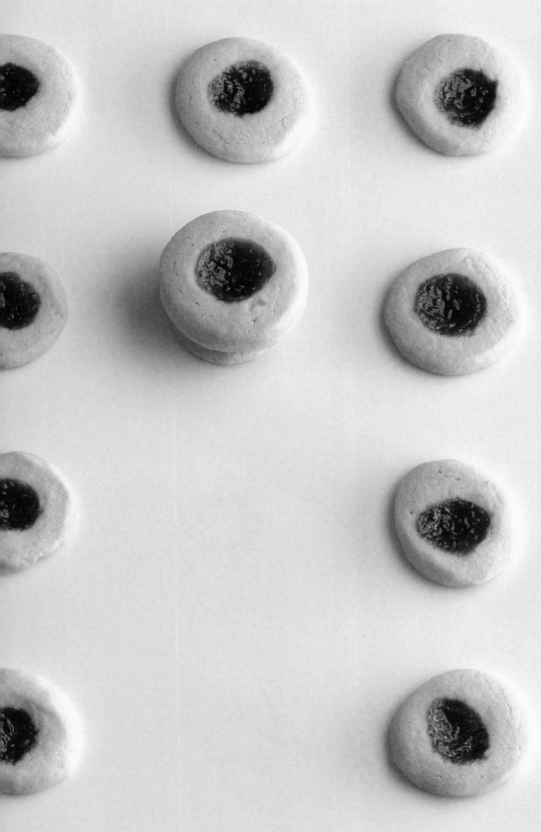

What to do:

1. Pre-heat the oven to 200°C.
2. Cream the butter and sugar until light and fluffy.
3. Mix the flour, potato flour and baking powder. Add this and the vanilla extract to the butter mixture and work into a dough.
4. Shape the dough into a length and cut into 24 pieces.
5. Roll the pieces into small balls and place them on a tray lined with baking paper, or into small paper cake cases.
6. Make a dent in each biscuit and add a dollop of jam.
7. Bake in the middle of the oven for 10-12 minutes. Sprinkle a little sifted icing sugar once cooled if desired.

Ingredients:

100 g cold butter

50 ml caster sugar

225-250 ml plain flour

1 drop bitter almond extract
 (optional)

Glaze and garnish:

egg white

nib sugar

almonds, finely chopped

1. Mix the butter, sugar, flour (start with 225 ml) and the bitter almond extract (if using). Quickly work into a smooth dough (a little more flour may be needed).

2. Ideally refrigerate the dough in cling film for about 30 minutes. Pre-heat the oven to 175°C.

3. Roll out the dough into equal finger-thick lengths.

4. Beat the egg white lightly with a fork and brush over the dough. Sprinkle with nib sugar and almonds. Cut all the lengths simultaneously into pieces 4-5 cm long. Place the fingers on a tray lined with baking paper.

5. Bake in the middle of the oven for around 10 minutes.

Ingredients:
100 g butter
2 tbsp caster sugar
200 ml plain flour
1 egg yolk

Filling:
50 g butter
  (room temperature)
100 ml caster sugar
150 ml (100 g) almonds,
  blanched, peeled and ground
2 eggs

Garnish:
200 ml icing sugar
1½ tbsp milk or water

12 ramekins
  or small foil cases

1. Quickly mix the butter, sugar and flour in a food processor or bowl. Add the egg yolk and mix it in. Wrap the dough in cling film and refrigerate for at least half an hour.

2. Pre-heat the oven to 175°C. Grease and flour the ramekins (foil cases won't need greasing or flouring).

3. Stir the ingredients for the filling into an even mixture.

4. Divide the sweet shortcrust pastry into 12 equal pieces. Press the pastry into the ramekins/cases with a floured thumb and put them on a tray. Add the filling.

5. Bake the mazarines in the middle of the oven for about 20 minutes until they start to colour nicely.

6. Mix the icing sugar and milk or water and stir into a smooth icing. Spread it onto the cakes once they're cold, or sift icing sugar over.

Ingredients:
200 g butter
1 egg
200 ml caster sugar
500-600 ml plain flour
½ tsp baking powder

Vanilla cream:
250 ml single cream
2 tbsp plain flour
1 tbsp sugar
1 egg + 1 egg yolk
3 drops vanilla extract
100 ml sweet apple sauce

Garnish:
icing sugar and cinnamon

small baking cases

1. Mix the butter, egg and sugar in a food processor. Add the flour mixed with baking powder.

2. Remove the dough and stand covered with cling film in the fridge for about half an hour.

3. Grease and flour the baking cases well.

4. Make the vanilla cream. Mix the cream, flour and sugar in a saucepan. Cook the mixture for about 3 minutes, stirring occasionally. Remove the pan from the heat and mix in the egg and egg yolk. Carefully heat the cream again for about half a minute. Leave to cool down a little and add the vanilla extract. Then leave to cool.

5. Divide the dough into four and use one piece at a time (leave the rest in the fridge).

6. Divide one piece of dough into 10 and press into the baking cases with a floured thumb.

7. Add a spoonful of vanilla cream and a spoonful of sweet apple sauce.

8. Take another piece of dough and roll it quite thinly. Make lids for the pastries and lay them on top of the filling. Press around the edges to make sure they attach. Pre-heat the oven to 200°C.

9. Form the rest of the dough into 20 or so pastries altogether.

10. Bake in the oven for about 8 minutes.

11. Leave to cool. Dust with a mixture of icing sugar and cinnamon.

Ingredients:

300 g marzipan

150 g butter
  (room temperature)

3 eggs

Filling:

100 g marzipan

orange liqueur or freshly
  squeezed orange juice

1 litre strawberries

lemon balm

What to do:

1. Pre-heat the oven to 175°C.

2. Grate the marzipan, add the butter and cream to a smooth paste. Add one egg at a time and mix to a smooth paste.

3. Spread out the mixture to an even layer about 1 cm thick in a small oven dish (about 25×25 cm) lined with baking paper. Bake in the middle of the oven for 12-16 minutes.

4. Let it cool and then cut into squares, or use cake cutters to make round or oval bases.

5. Grate the marzipan for the filling and add orange liqueur or freshly squeezed orange juice to taste, until a loose consistency is achieved.

6. Spread a layer of flavoured marzipan onto the bases.

7. Cut the strawberries length-ways and place densely on the marzipan. Garnish with lemon balm and maybe a small Swedish flag.

109

Ingredients:
3 sheets frozen puff pastry
250 ml custard
100 ml whipped cream
150 ml sweet apple sauce
3 tsp redcurrant jelly
100 ml icing sugar
½-1 tbsp water

What to do:

1. Semi-thaw the frozen puff pastry. Pre-heat the oven to 225°C.

2. Roll each sheet of pastry into a rectangle of 8×40 cm. Place on a baking tray that has been rinsed with water. Prick the sheets with a fork. Bake in the middle of the oven for around 10 minutes. Leave to cool. Trim to make the edges straight.

3. Make the custard and mix it with the whipped cream.

4. Spread sweet apple sauce onto one of the pastry bases. Add the next base on top.

5. Spread on quite a thick layer of custard.

6. Cover with the last base (bottom up).

7. Melt the jelly in the microwave and spread or brush on a thin layer.

8. Mix the icing sugar with the water, mix to a smooth icing and spread it over the jelly. Leave to set.

9. Cut the lengths into 10 slices.

113

Ingredients:

3 eggs

150 ml caster sugar

75 ml plain flour

75 ml potato flour

1 tsp baking powder

Filling:

150 ml milk

150 ml whipping cream

2 egg yolks

1 tbsp caster sugar

1 tbsp potato flour

4 gelatine leaves

200 ml whipping cream

2 drops vanilla extract

Garnish:

300 ml whipping cream

1 ready rolled disc of
  marzipan

icing sugar

marzipan rose

115

What to do:

1. Pre-heat the oven to 175°C. Grease a round springform cake tin, about 24 cm diameter, or line it with baking paper.

2. Beat the eggs and sugar until pale, light and fluffy.

3. Mix the flour, potato flour and baking powder and carefully stir this into the egg mix. Pour the mixture into the tin.

4. Bake in the bottom of the oven for around 30 minutes. Leave to stand for a few minutes before turning the cake out onto a cooling rack.

5. Filling: Mix the milk, the 150 ml of cream, egg yolks, sugar and potato flour for the filling in a saucepan. Heat over a low heat, stirring constantly, until the cream mixture has thickened and the first bubble appears. Remove the pan from the heat. Place the gelatine leaves in cold water for 5 minutes.

6. Remove the leaves from the water and place them in the warm cream mixture. Stir until the gelatine has melted.

7. Place the saucepan in cold water to cool the cream mixture, stirring occasionally.

8. Whip the new 200 ml of whipping cream with the vanilla extract into a firm foam. Add this whipped cream to the cream mixture.

9. Building the gateau and garnishing: Divide the cake into three bases. The top one should be about 1 cm thick. Place the bottom base onto a serving dish and spread on half the cream mixture.

10. Add the middle base and spread on the rest of the cream mixture. Make it slightly higher in the centre to make the gateau nicely rounded.

11. Place the final base on top. Whip the 300 ml of cream for the garnish. Spread a little cream around the edge and the rest on top of the gateau. Make it slightly higher towards the centre.

12. Cover with the marzipan disc. Garnish with icing sugar and a marzipan rose.

Ingredients:
3 eggs
100 ml caster sugar
50 ml potato flour
75 ml plain flour

Mousse:
200 ml whipping cream
4 gelatine leaves
1 egg
100 ml caster sugar
zest and juice of 1 lemon

Filling and garnish:
½ litre strawberries, 250 g
½ litre blueberries, 250 g
200 ml whipping cream
50 g toasted almond flakes
50 ml jelly sugar
50 ml water

What to do:

1. Pre-heat the oven to 200°C. Grease a round springform cake tin, about 24 cm diameter, or line it with baking paper.

2. Beat the eggs and sugar until very light and fluffy using an electric whisk over hot water to around 60°C. Remove the pan from the heat and continue whisking until the temperature decreases.

3. Sift the potato flour and flour into the egg mix. Pour the mixture into the tin.

4. Bake in the bottom of the oven for around 20 minutes. Leave to cool.

5. Mousse: Whip the cream and stand cold. Place the gelatine leaves in cold water for 5 minutes. Beat the egg and sugar until pale, light and fluffy. Add the lemon zest.

6. Pour the lemon juice into a saucepan. Take the gelatine leaves from the water and place them in the saucepan. Melt the gelatine over a low heat. Remove the pan from the heat. Stir a few tablespoons of the beaten egg mixture into the pan. Then stir the gelatine mixture into the rest of the egg mixture. Add the whipped cream.

7. Remove the cake from the tin and divide into 2 bases. Wash the tin and first place a layer of cardboard on the tin's base (for instance use a cake box; it provides stability when decorating the gateau). Cover the sides of the tin with baking paper or line the tin with cling film.

8. Place the bottom cake base back in the tin. Pour on half of the mousse mix. Slice half the strawberries and distribute them over the mousse along with half the blueberries.

9. Add the next base and pour on the rest of the mousse. Distribute whole strawberries and the rest of the blueberries on top.

10. Refrigerate for 1-2 hours. The gateau can also be frozen at this point.

11. Remove the gateau from its tin and transfer to a serving dish (leave the cardboard base where it is). Whip the cream and spread it around the sides of the gateau. Press in almonds.

12. Mix the jelly sugar and water in a saucepan and simmer for half a minute. Brush or spoon the warm jelly over the fruit.

Tip:
You can make an amazing raspberry gateau by replacing the lemon juice and zest in the mousse with 200 ml of fresh raspberries mashed up and mixed with sugar. Then fill and decorate the gateau with fresh raspberries.

Ingredients:
225 ml (150 g) hazelnuts
4 egg whites
175 ml caster sugar

Filling:
400-500 ml whipped cream
1 drop vanilla extract

Garnish:
cooking chocolate
cocoa powder

What to do:

1. If desired, toast the hazelnuts in a hot frying pan, transfer them to a towel and rub off the skins. Then grind them.

2. Pre-heat the oven to 150°C. Pour the egg whites into a fully clean and dry bowl. Beat the whites into a foam, but not as firm as for meringues.

3. Add the sugar and nuts and stir together gently.

4. Line two baking trays with baking paper. Draw two circles onto each tray, about 20 cm in diameter. Divide the mix into four and shape thinly and evenly into the circles. Bake in the middle of the oven for about 20 minutes.

5. Immediately detach the bases using a sharp knife and a non-stick palette knife, and leave them to cool on a rack.

6. Whip the cream, flavour with the vanilla extract and spread it over and between the bases.

7. Sift the cocoa over the gateau. Shave the cooking chocolate and sprinkle over the edge and top of the gateau, or garnish with chocolate pieces.

8. To make chocolate pieces, melt the cooking chocolate in the microwave or over a pan of simmering water. Spread the chocolate relatively thinly onto greaseproof paper and let it set. Cut into even pieces, as high as the gateau's edge, about 4-5 cm. Stand the chocolate pieces around the edge and on top of the cream – or use shavings on the top as pictured. Let the gateau stand cold until it's time to serve.

FIKA
Recipes for 30 baking classics.
From bite-size biscuits to festive cakes.

Project manager: Josefine Hallberg, IKEA Food Services AB
Project coordinator: Anders Truedsson, TITEL Books AB
Art Directors: Christoffer Persson & Staffan Lamm, Forsman & Bodenfors
Copywriter: Fredrik Jansson & Anders Hegerfors, Forsman & Bodenfors
Coordinator: Katarina Klofsten, Forsman & Bodenfors
Photography: Carl Kleiner/Mink Mgmt
Stylist: Evelina Kleiner
Recipes: Hembakningsrådet/www.hembakningsradet.se
Translation: Comactiva Translations AB, Sweden
Typesetting: Gyllene Snittet AB, Sweden

Produced by IKEA Food Services AB
Paper: Arcoset 140 g
Printing: Litopat S.p.A, Italy 2012